Tulip

Tulipa

Rose

Rosa

Helianthus

Papaver

Nymphaeaceae

Water Lily

Nymphaeaceae

Lilac

Syringa

Poppy

Papaver

Sunflower

Helianthus

Rose

Tulip

Tulipa

Dandelio

What Kind of Flower Are You, Little Girl?

Written by Nikki Holm

Illustrated by Heather Renaux

Ella,
May your true
self ever be cherished
+ nurtured as
the gift that
it is.

In light + in love,
Nikki
Holm

BEAVER'S
POND
PRESS

Cover and interior illustrations by Heather Renaux
Book design and typesetting by Tina Brackins

ISBN 13: 978-1-64343-742-2
Library of Congress Catalog Number: 2021912811

Printed in the United States of America
First Edition: 2022
26 25 24 23 22   5 4 3 2 1

Beaver's Pond Press
939 West Seventh Street
Saint Paul, MN 55102
(952) 829-8818
www.BeaversPondPress.com

MIX
Paper from
responsible sources
FSC® C008080

To order, visit www.withinthewave.com. Reseller discounts available.

Contact the author at www.withinthewave.com for school visits, speaking engagements, and interviews.

Photo by Kateland Steensgard

Nikki Holm is a board certified chaplain and spiritual director who has worked at the intersection of spiritual care and mental health for nearly a decade. Her most important calling, however, has been as a mom to two miraculous humans. This book was inspired by her experience accompanying countless women as they reconnect to their inherent worth while intentionally parenting her own children in hopes that they never question theirs. Nikki lives in Minnesota with her much-beloved family. To learn more visit www.withinthewave.com.

Heather Renaux is an illustrator and a folk-surrealist painter residing in Minneapolis, Minnesota. Her work is influenced deeply by nature, fairy tales, and the desire to never be bored. To see more, visit www.heatherrenaux.com.

To Miss Lydia Laine, for choosing to be mine and graciously teaching me how to be the mom you deserve each and every day. You truly are divinity embodied. I love you tons and bunches, little girl.

And to each and every one of my clients who wasn't nurtured in the way they needed or deserved. You too are divinity embodied. Hereafter, may you be cherished as the gems that you are!

—Nikki

To Christian, Billie, and Sophia: the world's most supportive husband and the two most incredibly magical little girls, who are now magical young women. My heart is yours.

—Heather

What kind of flower are you, little girl?

I want to know—
won't you tell me so?

Maybe you're a poppy,
who grows
ever so
wild.

Oh,
let me
cherish you,

my darling child.

Are you a water lily, who thrives away from land?

Show me what you need—
gently take my hand.

Could you be a tulip,
who persists
year
after
year?

Speak up, my love—

I am listening;
I am here.

Possibly you're a rose,

who has the means

to defend.

Tell me, sweet pea, how to you I best tend.

Perhaps you're a dandelion,
who freely
takes
up
space.

I'd be honored,
little light,
to help you
claim your place.

Might you be a lilac,
who radiates a
sweet, delightful scent?

Allow me to savor you;
that's my intent.

Perchance you're
a sunflower,
who stands
tall
above
the rest.

Please, my dear,
teach me how
to steward you best.

Oh, little girl,
lead me to care for

the seed
that is you.

Lest I give you
too much water
or too little sun,

too much trimming
or too little room,

guide me to
nurture the nature
that is true.

Please let me
nurture the nature
that is
you.

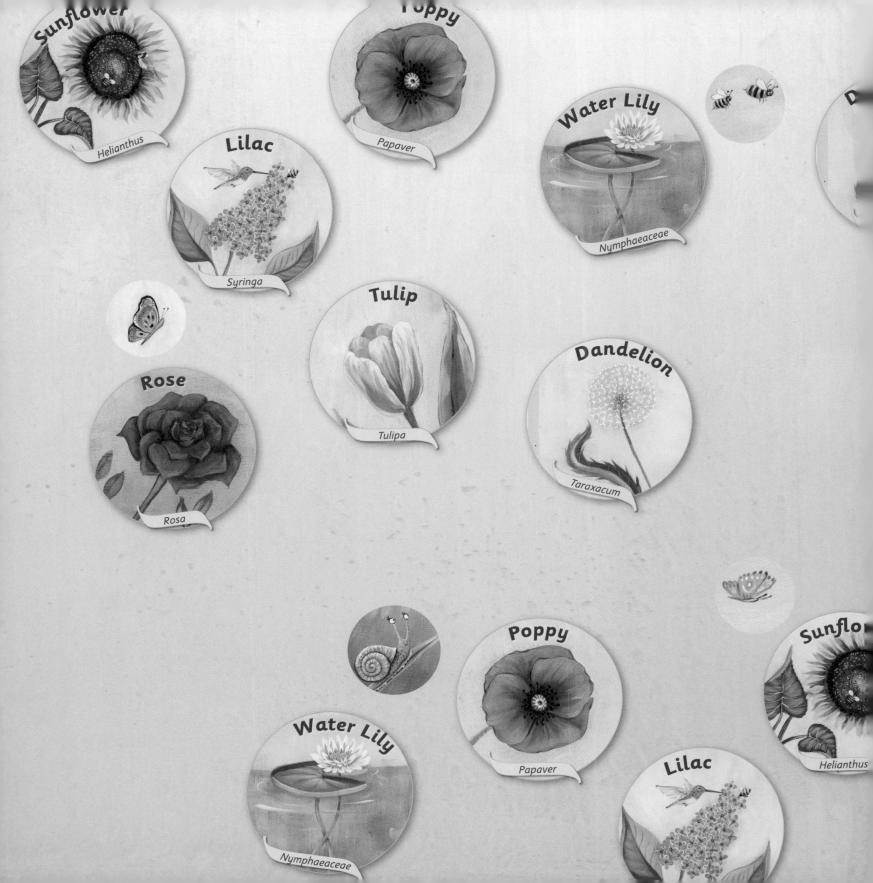